The Ultimate Animal Library

Bengal Tigers

by Chris Bowman

Blastoff! Readers 2

Bellwether Media • Minneapolis, MN

Blastoff! Readers are carefully developed by literacy experts to build reading stamina and move students toward fluency by combining standards-based content with developmentally appropriate text.

Level 1 provides the most support through repetition of high-frequency words, light text, predictable sentence patterns, and strong visual support.

Level 2 offers early readers a bit more challenge through varied sentences, increased text load, and text-supportive special features.

Level 3 advances early-fluent readers toward fluency through increased text load, less reliance on photos, advancing concepts, longer sentences, and more complex special features.

★ **Blastoff! Universe**

Reading Level

Grade K → Grades 1–3 → Grade 4

This edition first published in 2025 by Bellwether Media, Inc.

Library of Congress Cataloging-in-Publication Data

LC record for Bengal Tigers available at: https://lccn.loc.gov/2024012111

Editor: Elizabeth Neuenfeldt Series Designer: Veah Demmin

Printed in the United States of America, North Mankato, MN.

Table of Contents

What Are Bengal Tigers? 4
Powerful Predators 12
Growing Up 18
Glossary 22
To Learn More 23
Index 24

What Are Bengal Tigers?

Bengal tigers are big cats. Some are more than 10 feet (3 meters) long! These tigers call South Asia home.

Bengal Tiger Report

Range

Status in the Wild

Habitats

forests

grasslands

Bengal tigers are big **mammals**. They have wide necks and shoulders.

They have large paws and long claws. Their claws **extend** when tigers attack their **prey**.

Most Bengal tigers have orange **coats**. They have white fur on their bellies, necks, and faces.

Some Bengal tigers have mostly white fur.

Bengal tigers have black or brown stripes. Each tiger has its own pattern!

Their stripes help them hide while they hunt.

Spot a Bengal Tiger

Powerful Predators

Bengal tigers live in forests or **grasslands**. These **predators** live alone.

They claim their own **territory**.
They mark it with their **scent**.
This keeps other tigers away!

Bengal tigers are strong swimmers. Their powerful legs and large paws help them cross rivers.

Their sharp claws help them climb trees.

Bengal tigers usually hunt at night. They sneak up on prey. Then they **pounce**.

They often eat deer and antelope. They also eat wild boars.

Growing Up

Female Bengal tigers usually give birth to two to six **cubs** at a time.

Cubs learn to hunt from their mothers.

Cubs stay with their mothers for two or three years.

Adult females live near their mothers. Males often go find their own territory!

Life of a Bengal Tiger

Name of Babies

cubs

Number of Babies

2 to 6

Time Spent with Mom

2 or 3 years

Life Span

8 to 10 years

Glossary

coats–the fur or hair covering some animals

cubs–baby tigers

extend–to stretch out

grasslands–lands covered with grasses and other soft plants with few bushes or trees

mammals–warm-blooded animals that have backbones and feed their young milk

pounce–to suddenly jump on something to catch it

predators–animals that hunt other animals for food

prey–animals that are hunted by other animals for food

scent–an odor or smell

territory–the land area where an animal lives

To Learn More

AT THE LIBRARY

Feldman, Thea. *Tigers Can't Purr!: And Other Amazing Facts.* New York, N.Y.: Simon Spotlight, 2020.

Grack, Rachel. *Tigers.* Minneapolis, Minn.: Bellwether Media, 2022.

Scheffer, Janie. *African Lions.* Minneapolis, Minn.: Bellwether Media, 2025.

ON THE WEB

FACTSURFER

Factsurfer.com gives you a safe, fun way to find more information.

1. Go to www.factsurfer.com.
2. Enter "Bengal tigers" into the search box and click 🔍.
3. Select your book cover to see a list of related content.

Index

cats, 4
claws, 7, 15
climb, 15
coats, 8
colors, 8, 9, 10
cubs, 18, 20
females, 18, 21
food, 17
forests, 12
fur, 8, 9
grasslands, 12, 13
hunt, 10, 16, 18
legs, 14
life of a Bengal tiger, 21
males, 21
mammals, 6
mothers, 18, 20, 21
necks, 6, 8
night, 16
paws, 7, 14
pounce, 16
predators, 12
prey, 7, 16
range, 4, 5
rivers, 14
scent, 13
shoulders, 6
size, 4, 6, 7, 14
South Asia, 4
spot a Bengal tiger, 11
status, 5
stripes, 10
swimmers, 14
territory, 13, 21
trees, 15

The images in this book are reproduced through the courtesy of: InnaPoka, series patterns; Rene Holtslag, cover background, interior background; Denise Allison Coyle, cover (Bengal tiger); Berkah Visual, cover (tiger icon); KAMONRAT, p. 3; neelsky, p. 4; Sourabh Bharti, pp. 6, 8, 10-11; Dinodia, p. 7; Chaiwat Areeraksa, p. 9; andamanec, p. 10; Soonthorn Wongsaita, p. 11; ewastudio, p. 12; Photocech, pp. 13, 20; John Carnemolla, p. 14; armminivet, p. 15; julianwphoto, pp. 16-17; enciktat, p. 17 (tiger); Miroslav Serb, p. 17 (deer); Wirestock Creators, p. 17 (antelope); WildMedia, p. 17 (wild boars); pmvtisl, p. 18; Parikh Mahendra N, pp. 18-19; Anuradha Marwah, p. 21; Eric Isselee, p. 23.